ANXIETY WORKBOOK

BY LAURA MORRISSEY

THE HUMMINGBIRD CENTRE

ISBN: 978-1-9164-5609-9

Printed by IngramSpark

CONTENTS

INTRODUCTION

I have been working as a Counsellor for some time now and I would say that a constant theme for most of my clients is anxiety. For some this is unexplained, it is just how they have always been from a toddler onwards. For others there is an obvious trigger- a traumatic event, a loss of a loved one, a crime committed against them. These traumas can be worked through but in the meantime anxiety is invading their daily lives.

Anxiety is a small word and is often minimised, but for the person suffering from it, it can be crippling.

Upon searching the internet for solutions I discovered that there is a lot written on the subject but not enough simple interventions that a person can try, before seeking specialist help or medication.

I thought that it may be useful to share one of the tools that I have developed in my practice. I use it with adults and teenagers alike, sometimes as a starting point to alleviate distress and then deeper work follows on or sometimes this approach is enough.

This workbook gives control to the individual. They can see where things are going wrong for themselves and can then change things. I have found that change is the key to feeling better. Whether that be a change in behaviour or acceptance of the things out of their control, change is at the root of managing anxiety.

I have included some theory, but have deliberately not made this workbook too wordy. There are many books available on this subject and I will include some links if you desire more in depth knowledge but it is not essential to know all of the theories before using and benefitting from this book.

It can be used by you, no matter your age, or with you by a parent (if you allow it!), teacher, pastoral person or a counsellor. The worksheets can be copied and therefore used more than once.

The compass

Life is an intricate web of many interrelated parts that make the whole, the you. If one or more of these parts is out of balance or neglected completely then more often than not we feel unhappy, dissatisfied, out of kilter.

We know things feel wrong but are unsure why or how to make it better. This imbalance means that we use all sorts of coping mechanisms to self soothe. These are wide ranging and varied but here are a few examples:

• Avoid all social occasions
• Stay in your room/home
• Make your life shrink
• Self medicate with drink/drugs
• Stop doing things
• Self harm
• Give up

If we are able to identify which part is out of balance, then we can adjust it, a bit like balancing a wheel on a car. I have drawn up a 'Compass', with you at the centre and all your life parts on the circumference. I have identified 8 parts that make up a balanced life, each one represents the most important components of a persons life. One part or many may be out of alignment.

The parts are:

1. Home life
2. Educational or work life
3. Exercise
4. Diet
5. Sleep
6. Digital life
7. Creativity
8. Socialisation

The aim is to look at each 'part' in depth, see how you now feed it or starve it.

The next stage is to collect ideas about how that part of you could be nurtured and then you plan for how to address the missing elements.

Each part is taken in turn and can be worked on over the course of a week or a number of sessions. It is up to you!

"Anxiety is now recognised as one of the most prevalent mental health problems in the UK, yet there is good evidence that it is still underreported, under-diagnosed and under-treated." [1]

The Theory! What is Anxiety?

Anxiety is a normal part of our life. It makes us try harder, get up, go for that interview, study for that exam. Stress is a modern day plague but it stems from our early history as 'cave people'.

Our internal systems were developed to keep us safe, recognise, deal with or avoid threats to our existence when we were at real risk from attack. We would become hyper aware of our surroundings, the heart rate increased by adrenaline being poured through our bodies. The major muscle groups would receive more oxygen by the increased blood flow, readying us for the 'Flight, Fight, Freeze or Flop' response required to help us survive threats. Many feel butterflies in their stomachs or tingling in their extremities as the first indication of this spike in adrenaline and increase in blood flow. The food in the stomach is left undigested as this is not needed in time of threat.

The body produces cortisol when under threat, allowing for explosive action, to run, to fight. Adrenaline and cortisol act together. Adrenaline speeds up the heart rate and increases energy, cortisol promotes glucose to be released into you blood. This is the fuel. Cortisol also suppresses the digestive and the immune system. Too much cortisol over too long a time period increases the risk of becoming depressed, obese, heart disease, digestive problems, sleep disruption. All too often this response is triggered but the cortisol is not utilised or metabolised, in effect our bodies over reacted.

These natural body held responses are kicked in with everyday situations that are not putting our lives in jeopardy, our body is in overdrive.

One way of imaging what is happening in our bodies is to think of a cup of coffee. There are usually dregs left after we have finished our drink. If we leave the dregs but top up the coffee, eventually we will, over time have a cup full of unpleasant coffee. As we keep on going in this manner, eventually it will take very little to make the cup overflow. This is us filling up our cup or body with chemicals every time we respond to minor stressors but fail to use them for the purpose are designed for or discharging them via other outlets, such as exercise.

This means that the effect of stress is cumulative and why we may react to a seemingly trivial trigger such as being late for a meeting or dropping something. It makes our cup overflow and we do this too often, too extremely, too damaging a manner for ourselves or others.

We need to develop ways of rinsing the cup out after each drink, not allowing the sediment to take over, to ruin the coffee. Activities such as exercise, meditation, yoga, reading, baking, knitting all help us rinse out our cups or develop a spigot that siphons out the detritus of our day on a regular basis, a bit like a tap on a water collecting barrel.

Anxiety can produce physical, psychological and/or behavioural responses.

Common physical effects can be:

• Increase in the heart rate
• Wobbly legs
• Tingling hands/feet
• Hard to breathe
• Headaches
• Sweating
• Lack of saliva
• Feeling like you are choking
• Feel like you will pass out
• Wanting to go to the loo more often
• Sickness

This can effect our thinking:

• I'm going to die, I am having a heart attack
• I must escape
• I can't concentrate
• I have gone blank
• I have a feeling of being separated from what is actually occurring

This prompts us to try and find ways of behaving that stop these feelings that are so uncomfortable. Panic takes over as we try to avoid the sensations. People begin to refuse to go out of the house, on the bus, to school. They refuse to go into examination halls, their life becomes smaller. The immediate effect of avoiding the feeling or situation that created it, is that the body will calm down, feel less threatened. This then becomes the message that when your body feels anxious, the answer is to avoid the stimulus. This becomes your behavioural blueprint, that becomes more entrenched every time it is enacted, weaving a thread through every situation that creates feelings of anxiety - your body screams, "I must avoid it".

This is the Anxiety Compass!

The idea is to look at your life and work out what your priorities are, for you! Which part of your life is out of balance?

Start wherever makes sense to you, miss sections out that feel balanced already or complete the whole compass - it is up to you!

Remember, goals change, revise, adapt and set new destinations. Use the prompts or make up your own.

For each section there are 3 worksheets

Sheet 1: The first step is to look at the situation as of now, how much do you currently do, sleep, eat....Be honest! Nobody is checking, only you.

Sheet 2: Then on this sheet, dream away. What would a more balanced you look like? What would you be doing? Achieving?

Sheet 3: This is where you set REALISTIC goals. Break goals down into short, medium & long term. In the short term just deciding to change something that is not working can be empowering in itself.

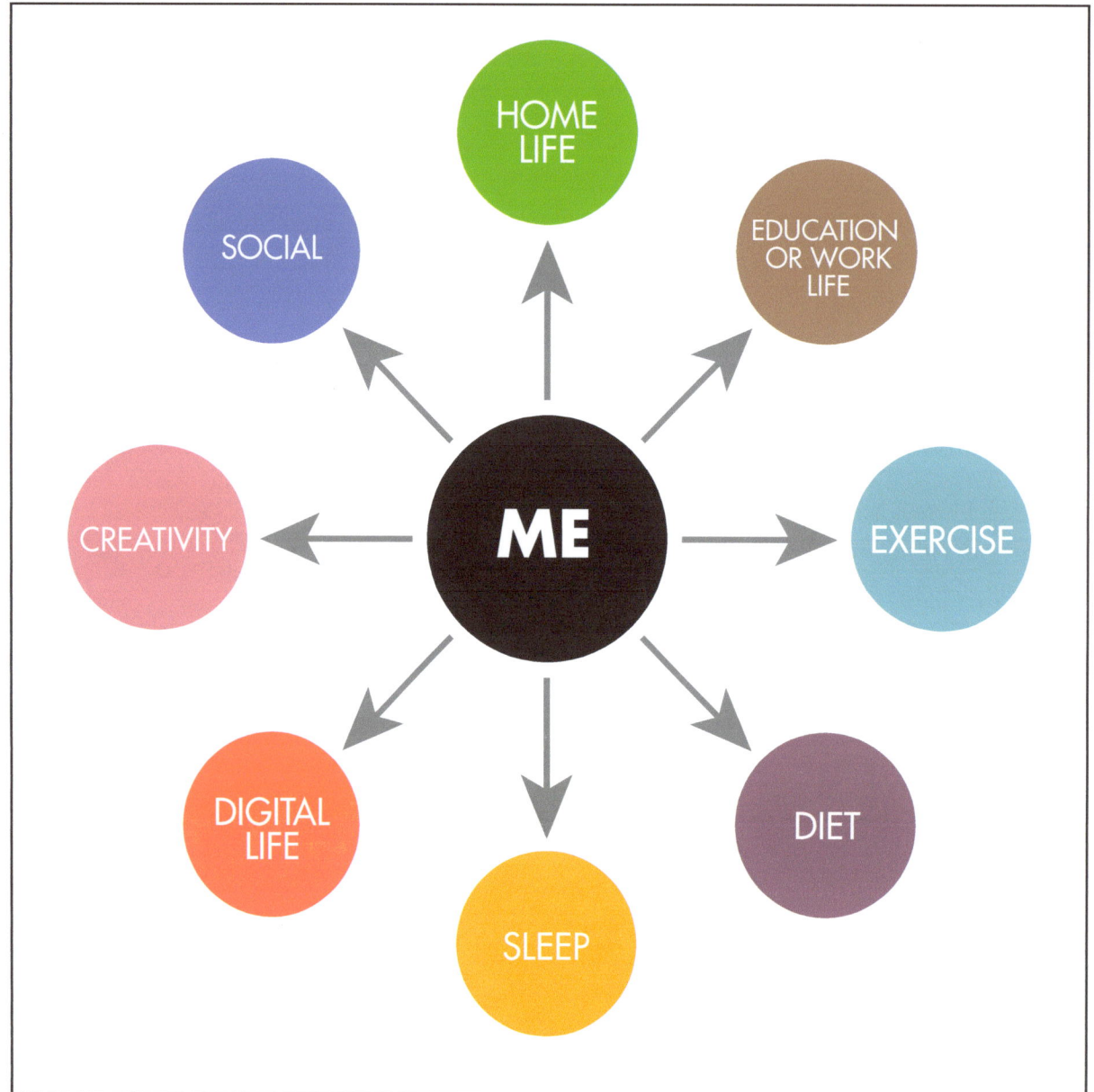

SOCIAL

HOME LIFE

EDUCATION OR WORK LIFE

CREATIVITY

ME

EXERCISE

DIGITAL LIFE

SLEEP

DIET

ANXIETY WORKBOOK - © LAURA MORRISSEY - THE HUMMINGBIRD CENTRE

HOME LIFE

HOME LIFE

Families are complex. Media portrays the idyll, smiling families with 2.4 children, happy, wealthy, often living by the sea in an amazing house. The reality for many is starkly different.

Understanding your family dynamics and personalities can help you understand yourself.

Anxiety does not like to be alone, it feeds off others peoples anxious thoughts and actions. It is all too easy to gathers the traits from those around us, influencing us. Anxious young people often have anxious parents, it becomes the family script "we are all anxious in our family".

In addition to this is the fact that not all families are supportive, living together or indeed in contact. These realities cannot be altered but can perhaps be accepted rather than railed against. If a family is too dysfunctional then support may be needed from external people.

It can be useful to identify who, if anyone in your family is a calming influence and encourage spending more time together.

Families can support you with anxiety in many cases but often they need to know how to actually help! The Calm Clinic has a list of how families can help, and things not to do! [14]

The Calm Clinic includes things such as:

- Let the person talk
- Stay calm
- Don't catch their anxiety!
- Be forgiving
- Don't expect them to be able change overnight
- Plan trips & family experience

What are my close relationship & who are they with?

Who can I laugh with?

Who can I talk to?

Who makes me feel angry/sad...?

Who do I miss?

Dream Sheet:

How would I like my family to be? How would I like my friendships to be?

What relationship can I improve this week?

What can I change over the next 4 weeks?

What relationship can I accept as it is?

How do I want my family & friendships to look in year & how can I achieve this

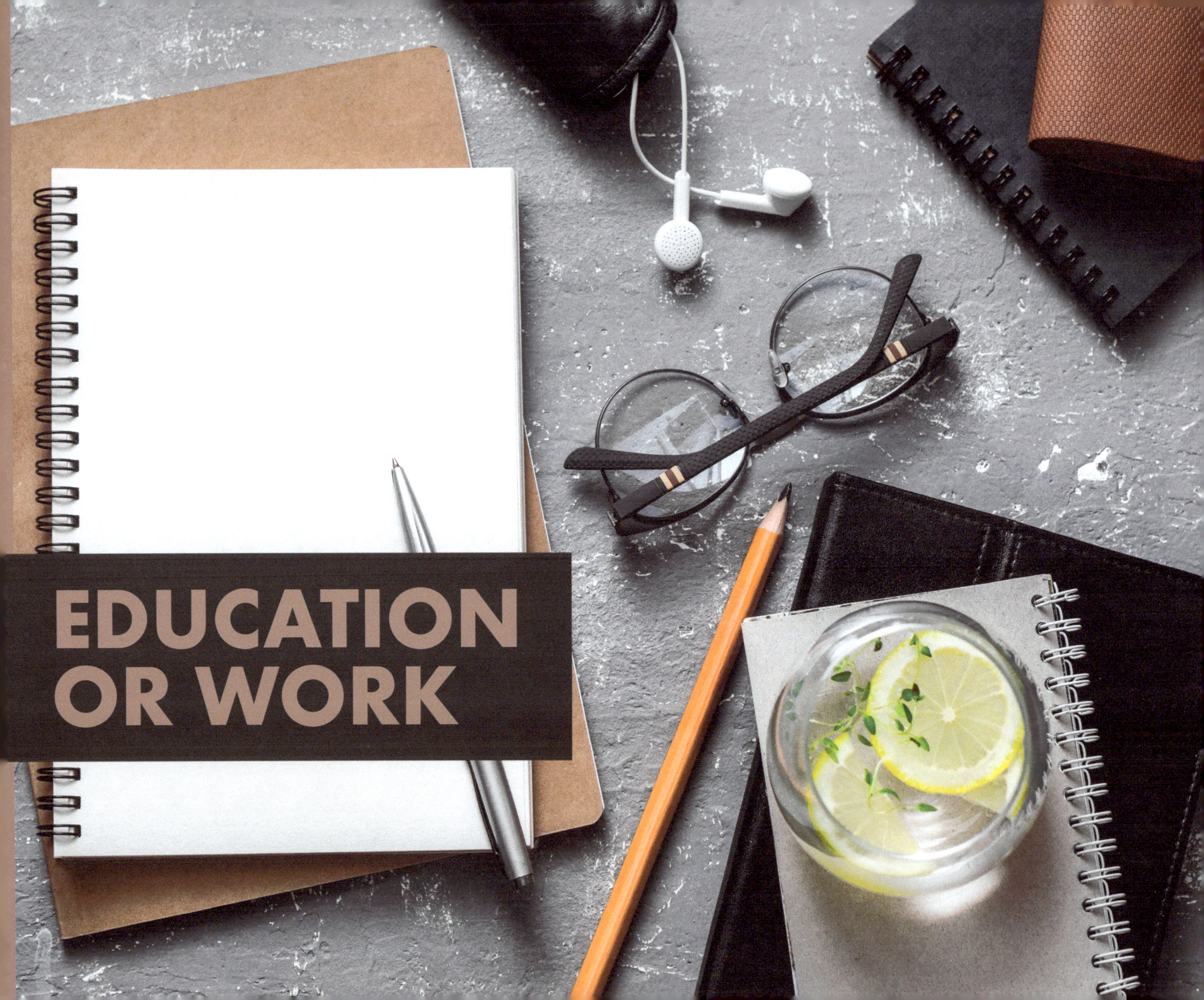

EDUCATION OR WORK

EDUCATION OR WORK

Anxiety and stress can affect the ability to perform at school or work. It can make us not want to go into school, college or work. Missing school has a massive impact on our ability to achieve academically. Missing work will often result in disciplinary warnings and possibly dismissal.

Wanting to achieve can make us anxious but it is likely that depression affects academic achievement not the other way around.

It affects ability to socialise, perform well and concentration. Anxiety can make people too scared to go into examinations, make them 'go blank' and fail to get their knowledge out onto the exam paper. Fear prevents us doing well and this effects future career goals. This fear and anxiety, unless dealt with, can follow us throughout our lives, stopping us achieving our full potential. This can also lead to depression.[8]

Anxiety in the workplace can lead to the need to take time off work. Often this is not viewed kindly by employers. This in itself causes an additional layer of stress, the individual may try and conceal their anxiety for fear of judgement.

Anxiety can certainly effect the ability to think at work, to be clear, and manage deadlines, in some people.

The key is to build up support networks with colleagues, other students, family.

Identify key stressors:

- Is the job the right job for you?
- Is your boss the issue?
- Become an excellent time manager
- Establish boundaries
- Learn to say no, constructively
- Perfection does not exist!
- Be honest about things that you get wrong and change i.e be on time!

https://www.helpguide.org/articles/stress/stress-in-theworkplace. htm

What are you doing now?

What is working well?

What is not working?

Dream Sheet:

Using images, words think about what your work/education would look like?

Goals

Short Term: What can I do this week?

Medium Term: What can I change over the next 4 weeks?

Long Term: Where do I see myself in a year? & how can I get there?

EXERCISE

EXERCISE

Cortisol can be damaging to our overall health if it not dealt with in a positive way. Cortisol is naturally produced when we exercise but the levels quickly return to normal after the session ends. Regularly exercising reduces the amount of cortisol in our blood stream. This helps reduce stress and help us to manage the negative effects of this chemical.

Physical activity has a positive effect on our mood and improves our general wellbeing. Even short bursts of activity, 10 minutes brisk walking, improves our energy levels, our mood and our ability to think more clearly [2]

More research is needed to identify the best form of exercise but it is believed that aerobic exercise has the most positive impact, equally walking briskly can really help shift a mood from negative to positive.

Taking part in physical activity can improve our self esteem [3] and reduce stress [4], thus helping to stave off the development of mental health problems [5]. It improves the quality of our lives [6]. It can show us measurable improvements that we can reflect on and this improves our feelings of self worth.

Regular exercise can improve our body shape, our body confidence and can improve our lung efficiency and our auto immune system, thus benefitting our general health as well as our mental wellbeing.

The advice is to always check with your GP before embarking upon a new exercise regime.

"Exercise can reduce your risk of major illnesses, such as heart disease, stroke, type 2 diabetes and cancer by 50% and lower the risk of early death by 30%" [7]

How often do I exercise?

Why did it stop?

What exercise do I currently do?

How did I feel after exercise?

What exercise did I used to do & have now stopped

Dream Sheet:

What would I like to do? How would I like to feel or look? (use images if it helps, or words...)

 ANXIETY WORKBOOK · © LAURA MORRISSEY · THE HUMMINGBIRD CENTRE

Goals

Short Term: What will I do this week?

Medium Term: What will I do this month

Long Term: What will I continue doing?

DIET

DIET

Diet effects how you feel, it may not cause anxiety but it can exacerbate it or assist in it's management.

A healthy diet helps to ensure that surges in energy and the subsequent slumps are smoothed out. If you eat a sugary, fat fuelled doughnut, your energy will soar - for a short time and then the crash happens. This up and down in our energy levels effect how we feel. You will probably recognise the after dinner slump of a white carbohydrate meal (i.e pasta) if it is eaten at lunchtime? The afternoon is one long struggle to stay awake. By eating more protein at lunch and wholegrains it can make us more awake after lunchtime, vital if we are in education or meetings that go on...

Foods to avoid/reduce:

- Sugary foods
- Processed foods
- Caffeine
- Alcohol
- Acid forming foods such as yogurts, eggs, sour cream. It is believed that they reduce magnesium levels, a contributory factor in anxiety [12]
- Dairy products - can increase adrenaline levels, thus making you feel anxious

Diet effects our overall well being, and eating the foods below should reduce anxiety levels.

What to eat:

- Fruit & vegetables
- Water
- Tryptophan rich foods (i.e oats, soy, poultry etc)
- Magnesium rich foods (Black beans, tofu)
- Omega 3 Fatty Acids (Fish, flax seeds, squash).

Do I eat regular meals?

Does my weight& energy levels fluctuate?

How much sugar & salt do I consume on a daily basis?

Am I ill a lot?

Do I have a balanced diet?

Do I struggle to concentrate?

Do I eat fruit & vegetables at every meal?

Am I always tired?

Dream Sheet:

What do I want to feel like? Look like?

Goals

Short Term: What can I change this week?

Medium Term: What can I change over the next 4 weeks?

Long Term: How will I feel/look like in a year & how can I get there?

SLEEP

SLEEP

Anxiety stops us sleeping, that feeling of being tired but when our head hits the pillow, our minds go into overdrive.

The mind pursues one loop of worry, then another and then back again. Lists, things to do, things that have been said or left unsaid race through minds. Then constantly seeing the clock moving inexorably on, minute upon minute, hour upon hour then heightens the feeling of anxiety making it harder to sleep than ever. Fear of not being able to sleep prevents sleep! This can then lead onto anxiety disorders, and medical help may be needed if the problem is chronic.

However, there are some simple strategies that can help!

1. Meditation

This is a great discipline and you cannot 'fail'. Even if the meditative state is hard to manage, just recognise your thoughts and return to the meditation. It can take time to learn this skill but can then be utilised throughout your life, allowing you to acquire a sense of calm in any situation. There are many apps available or even just listening to white noise or rain on a roof can be meditative. Find what suits you.

2. Exercise

If you regularly exercise, you sleep better but maybe look at not being too aerobic late in the evening.

3. Bedtime routine

About an hour before you think you want to sleep, think relaxation! Have a warm bath or shower, get comfortable. Dim the lights, turn off electronics, have a warm drink. Get ready for bed.

4. Lists!

Use a pad to write down any worries that you may have, but don't want to forget in the morning. Writing them down gives you the security of knowing that you will remember it in the morning and do not have to keep remembering it all night.

5. Write it down!

Journalling is a great way of managing anxiety. Write down all your thoughts, then capture 3 thing you are grateful for in the day. Next write down one thing that you can do differently.

6. Worry Time

Set time aside to write, to worry and limit the time, trying not to let anxiety flood you the rest of the day

ANXIETY WORKBOOK · © LAURA MORRISSEY - THE HUMMINGBIRD CENTRE

Record current sleep patterns

Am I always tired?

Do I get at least 7/8 hrs sleep a night or 13 if a teenager?

How does this effect my mood?

Dream Sheet:

How would I like to feel? How much sleep do I need?

Goals

Short Term: What can I change this week?

Medium Term: What can I change over the next 4 weeks?

Long Term: What will my sleep pattern look like in a year & how can I get there?

DIGITAL LIFE

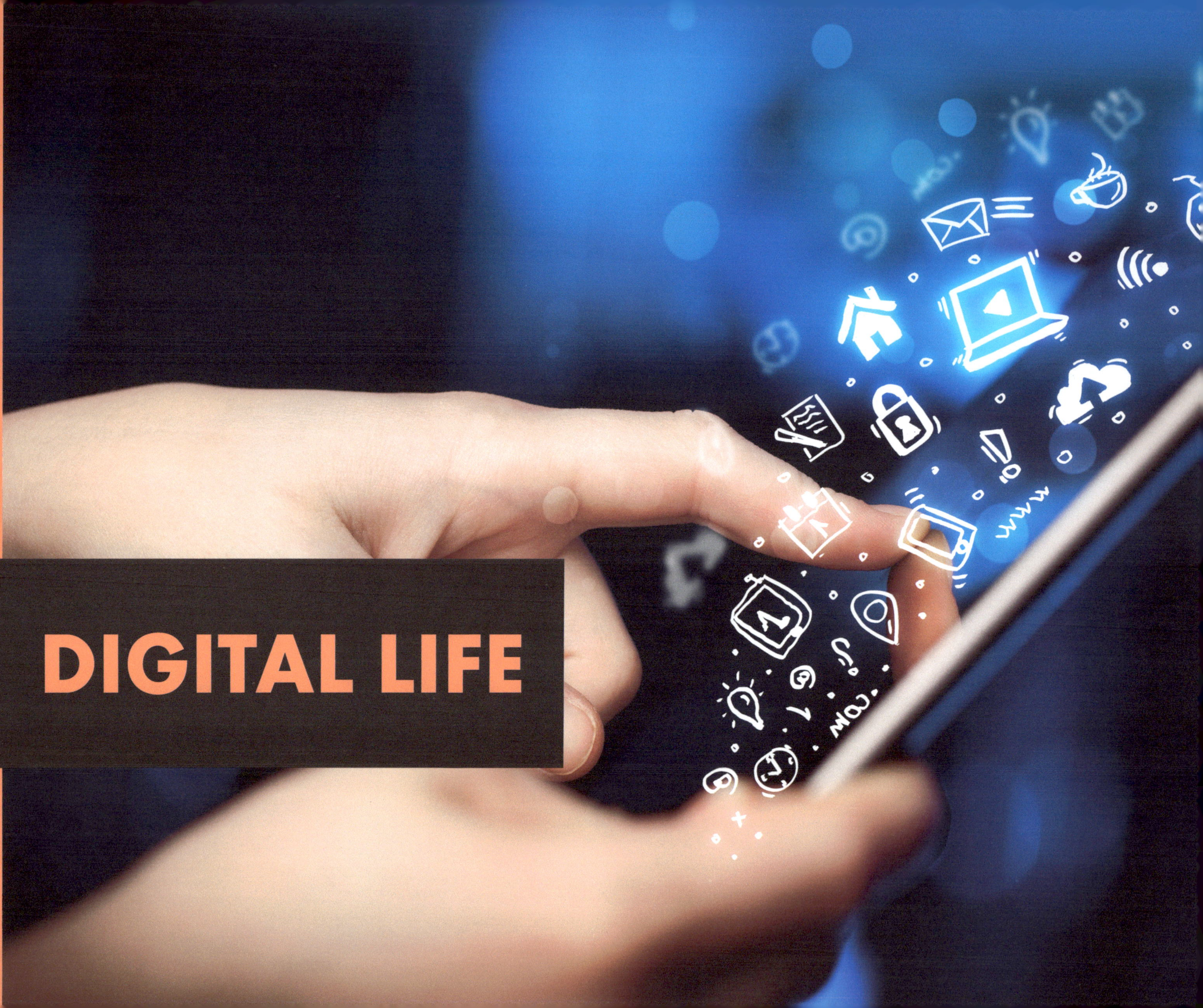

DIGITAL LIFE

The average person is spending 25 hours online a week [9] Teenagers are attached to their phones as if their very life was at risk should they lose it.

The evidence on technology and anxiety is contradictory. Most indicate that some limits should be set but guidance is lacking and is often not supported by research.

The evidence that I see every day is that adults and children are constantly connected to the web, to social networking sites. People walk and text at the same time, oblivious to others in their path.

Restaurants have most tables occupied by couples or families all looking at their own devices - maybe sharing a photo or stream with each other. They talk more to those not present than they do to those they are sharing their meal with.

Teenagers spend most of their time in their rooms, on their own, accessing the wider world virtually. They do not interact with their family. They no longer need to access the family television in the lounge because they can watch whatever they want to at any time.

Adults are as guilty as their teens. They constantly thumb through their social media whilst criticising their offspring for doing just that. They use gadgets as a childminding instrument, much as the TV used to be used in other generations.

Anxiety can be increased by the type of social media used and this is also determined by your own personality type. Do you compare yourselves with the images you consume, do you feel better or worse when you have come off the social media platform? Only you know how it genuinely impacts on how you feel about yourself.

Some high profile Hollywood stars refuse to use social media. Jennifer Lawrence does not use Twitter, Facebook or Instagram. Sandra Bullock does not take selfies as she believes that they give a 'false projection of our lives'. No one posts a selfie or picture that shows them being vile to their mother or children. Ed Sheeran does not own a phone!

There is advice about turning tech off an hour before going to bed. The blue light emitted by the screens from our gadgets suppress the production of melatonin. Melatonin controls our sleep cycle and a reduction in melatonin makes it harder to fall and stay asleep. The brain is stimulated by social media and fails to recognise it is time to sleep. [10]

Solutions to Technology-Induced Insomnia [11]

Thankfully, there are measures we can take to reduce the sleepdepriving effects that blue lights have on us. Here are six solutions that will help:

1. Dim the light on the screen as evening approaches. In fact, dimming all the lights in the house will send a signal from the eye to the brain that it's time to start preparing for the sleep cycle.

2. Install an app on your phone that warms up the colours during the evening. This app causes the light on the screen to shift from the short-wave blue spectrum to the longer red and yellow wavelength.

3. Invest in a pair of blue-light filtering eyeglasses. You will still be able to see but filtering out the blue light spectrum can help trigger the pineal gland to start producing melatonin.

4. At least one to two hours before a set bedtime, power down all bluelight devices in the house, including TVs, computers, tablets and smartphones. This will help trigger the production of melatonin and sleepiness will set in at the right time.

5. Install as many full spectrum lights in your home as possible. Couple this with installing the smart-home feature that gradually dims the all the lights throughout the home, beginning at sunset. This will imitate the setting of the sun and the body will react accordingly.

6. Avoid using energy-efficient blue lights in night lights located in bedrooms, hallways, and bathrooms. Instead, use bulbs with a warmer hue, such as dim red lights, which have higher wavelengths that do not inhibit the pineal gland's secretion of melatonin.

How long am I honestly on my phone/tablet etc a day?

Would I panic if there was no coverage?

Am I always checking my phone even when out with someone?

How do I feel after coming of the sites I use regularly?

Dream Sheet:

How do I want to live? How would life look if I managed my tech life better?

Goals

Short Term: What can I change this week?

Medium Term: What can I change over the next 4 weeks?

Long Term: What will my use of technology look like in a year

CREATIVITY

CREATIVITY

It could be argued that the creative and gifted amongst us, can also be the most tortured souls. Comedians talk of depression, artists struggle with never being good enough.

However, for the rest of us, creativity can help with anxiety. Stand up comedy is a method used to address anxiety. If you doodle, hum, write journals, then that is all good! Engaging in art, theatre, dance, photography, writing is also good for your health, it reduces anxiety. Music can affect mood, quickly.

Many of the clients I see with anxiety have lost their creative outlet. Due to time, work, family commitments, their muse has disappeared. Their life feels dull, monochromatic. Their creativity gave them time to use their right side of the brain, to step out of the here and now and dream. Switch their brain off from the boring and enter a world of colour - even if for a short time.

Creativity feeds us and allows us to express our feelings through different mediums.

As psychologist Elaine Slater explains: 'This can put us in a near meditative state where we lose track of time and feel removed from the stressors of life.' [9]

Perhaps this downtime can help us problem solve. Famous people in history such as Churchill (painted) and Einstein (played piano and violin) had creative outlets as well as their serious jobs as world leader and physicist.

Creativity can be a form of mindfulness. A rest from the humdrum!

Creativity allows us to think outside the box, be more childlike because there is no right or wrong. It does not have to be perfect. We do it just because it makes us feel good.

What do I do now that is creative?

What did I used to enjoy?

Dream Sheet:

Use images, words... Creativity can be drawing, writing, baking, gardening...

Goals

Short Term: What can I change now?

Medium Term: What can I change over the next 4 weeks?

Long Term: What do I want it to look like in a year, & how do I get there?

SOCIALISATION

SOCIALISATION

"Adequate amounts of social support are associated with increases in levels of a hormone called oxytocin, which functions to decrease anxiety levels and stimulate the parasympathetic nervous system calming down responses" [13]

We are social beings. The need to belong to our 'tribe' is part of our makeup.

Establishing and maintaining a sense of belonging helps reduce our stress, as it promotes a sense of belonging, being seen, heard and makes us feel safe. It has many benefits including how long we live, improving our physical health, improving our immune system and reducing the risk of dementia. It also impacts on our mental health in a positive way, making us feel more connected, improves our mood and builds a sense of belonging.

The hormone Oxytocin also promotes a desire to seek more contact with others, thus perpetuating the socialisation cycle.

Socialisation by it's very nature makes us think outwards rather than always looking inside ourselves. It encourages communication and mutual support, giving life more meaning.

Socialisation can take the form of:

- Mixing with family & Friends
- Neighbours
- Volunteering because altruistic acts activate neurotransmitters that are associated with positivity
- Clubs
- Exercise

How much do I socialise now?

How has this made me feel?

Do I enjoy the social things that I do?

Why did I stop?

Have I stopped socialising?

Dream Sheet:

How would I life my social life to look?.

Goals

Short Term: What can I change this week?

Medium Term: What can I change over the next 4 weeks?

Long Term: How do I want my social life to look in a year & how can I get there?

REFERENCES

References

(1) https://www.mentalhealth.org.uk/sites/default/files/living-with-anxiety-report.pdf

(2) Ekkekakis, P., Hall, E.E., Van Landuyt, L.M. & Petruzzello, S. (2000). Walking in (affective) circles: Can short walks enhance affect?

(3) Ifermann, D. & Stoll, O. (2000). Effects of Physical Exercise on Self-Concept and Wellbeing. International Journal of Sport Psychology, 31, 47–65.

(4) Salmon, P. (2001). Effects of Physical Activity on Anxiety, Depression, and Sensitivity to Stress: A Unifying Theory. Clinical Psychology Review, 21 (1), 33–61.

(5) Zschucke, E., Gaudlitz, K. & Strohle, A. (2013). Exercise and Physical Activity in Mental Disorders: Clinical and Experimental Evidence. J Prev Med Public Health, 46 (1), 512– 521.

(6) Alexandratos, K., Barnett, F. & Thomas, Y. (2012). The impact of exercise on the mental health and quality of life of people with severe mental illness: a critical review. British Journal of Occupational Therapy, 75 (2), 48–60.

(7) https://www.nhs.uk/Livewell/fitness/Pages/whybeactive.aspx (Retrieved 13.08 on 8/11/17)

(8) https://www.intechopen.com/books/a-fresh-look-at-anxiety-disorders/impact-of-anxietyand- depression-symptoms-on-scholar-performance-in-high-school-and-university-stude

(9) http://balance.media/issues/benefits-of-creativity/

(10) https://sleep.org/articles/ways-technology-affects-sleep/

(11) https://channels.theinnovationenterprise.com/articles/the-connection-betweentechnology- and-insomnia

(12) https://www.calmclinic.com/anxiety/treatment/diet

(13) https://www.mentalhelp.net/articles/socialization-and-altruistic-acts-as-stress-relief/

(14) https://www.calmclinic.com/anxiety/tips-for-friends-family

Useful Organisations

anxietyuk.org.uk

calmer-you.com

Mental health helplines - NHS.UK

nopanic.org.uk

sleepfoundation.org

youngminds.org.uk